© 2020 Stacy Savary

All Rights Reserved. No portion of this book may be reproduced, stored in a retrieval system, or transmitted in any form or by any means - electronic, mechanical, photocopy, recording, scanning, or other - except for brief quotations in critical reviews or articles, without the prior written permission of the publisher.

Published by Daughter of the King Publishing, Orlando, FL

ISBN: 979-8558506532

Note: *Endometriosis News is strictly a news and information website about the disease. It does not provide medical advice, diagnosis, or treatment. This content is not intended to be a substitute for professional medical advice, diagnosis, or treatment. Always seek the advice of your physician or other qualified health provider with any questions you may have regarding a medical condition. Never disregard professional medical advice or delay in seeking it because of something you have read on this website. The opinions expressed in this column are not those of Endometriosis News or its parent company, BioNews Services, and are intended to spark discussion about issues pertaining to endometriosis.*

TABLE OF CONTENTS

FOREWARD - by Rev. Darrin Lindsay

DEDICATION

CHAPTER 1 - A Storm is Brewing

CHAPTER 2 - Clear Skies, Calm at Sea

CHAPTER 3 - Watch Out For Sharks

CHAPTER 4 - Drowning, Someone Rescue Me

CHAPTER 5 - Clinging to the Rock

CHAPTER 6 - The Perfect Storm to Take Me Out

CHAPTER 7 - The Eye of the Storm

Foreward by Rev. Darrin Lindsay

Blessed is the person who keeps on going when times are hard. After they have come through hard times, this person will receive a crown. The crown is life itself. The Lord has promised it to those who love him.

– James 1:12 (NIRV)

I've known Stacy since 2005. We met while working as local missionaries with Youth Unlimited in Toronto, serving young people in marginalized communities. Stacy's passion for life was and is evident to anyone she meets, and deeply impacted the students she was mentoring. Her energy and enthusiasm deeply impacted the staff at YU, including me. As a result, our relationship has changed from colleagues to friends. So I can say, it is impossible to know Stacy, and not know that Jesus was the source of her joy.

As a pastor, I've met a lot of joyful people. And I've also walked with a lot of people through the storms of life. It's relatively easy to be joyful when life is going well. However, it's rare to meet someone, even a believer, that exudes joy in the midst of suffering. Stacy Savary is one of those people!

She embodies the kind of faith that Jesus' brother James describes in his letter quoted above. Faith that perseveres in the face of trials of many kinds. Faith that asks God for wisdom. Faith that recognizes every good and perfect gift comes from our Heavenly Father. Faith that isn't blown and tossed around by the winds of the storm.

I'm so pleased my friend Stacy has shared her intensely personal story in *The Perfect Storm*. That she has written intimately about her struggles with relationships, health and discrimination is going to be helpful for many living with pain of all kinds. In fact, I believe it will be a source of encouragement and inspiration for anyone that reads it.

Book Dedication

This book is dedicated to my mother, a true Warrior and the glue to our family. Thank you for your grace, your mercy and for not giving up on me, even when I caused so much pain. I thank God for redeeming our relationship in this process. Thank you to my other family members and siblings.

This book is also dedicated to my son; I wasn't courageous enough to fight for you, but if I can help to save others then your life was not in vain...

I can do all things through Christ who strengthens me.
Philippians 4:13

STACY SAVARY

Stacy Savary Biography

For over 21 years, Stacy Savary has been a noteworthy leader within her community, providing social support and outreach, especially within the Caribbean community. She has provided services at homeless shelters, grassroot organizations, children's camps, mentoring programs and outreach events for at-risk youth in disenfranchised areas in Toronto, Ontario, Canada.

Stacy has always had a passion of working with marginalized groups, specifically women and youth groups. While she has a passion to help others, she has also faced numerous health challenges that required her to seek healing for herself. She was diagnosed with Endometriosis, a disorder where the tissue that makes up the uterine lining (the lining of the womb) grows outside the uterus. Endometriosis is usually found in the ovaries, Fallopian tubes and the tissue lining your pelvis.

Despite her challenges, Stacy vowed to maintain a positive, balanced and fulfilling outlook on life. Through all her pain, struggles in dealing with the health issues, along with her commitment to her career as a Social Worker, Stacy decided to share her life's journey through this book, in hopes to inspire and empower others to navigate through the storms of life no matter how messy the waters maybe.

Chapter 1 - A Storm is Brewing

I was a late-bloomer. As a child, most of the girls between the ages of ten to thirteen in my grade, had their periods. I was the last one to "develop", meaning go through puberty, in elementary school — so, according to everyone else I was a "late-bloomer." I saw what my friends had to go through back then as we would share little secrets in the gym and locker room. So, I knew by the time I had started my period, I would be prepared, because I thought that I had the knowledge and skills. How hard would it be to learn how to insert a tampon or put on a maxi pad? Not rocket science! Unfortunately for me, it was a little bit tricky and very messy from the start.

The day my period started, I was playing at home, and I started to feel very sick. My grandmother was taking care of us that day. I was horrified that not only was I wearing white shorts, I had soiled my pants. I remember going to my grandmother, crying because I thought I was going to die. I told her that I was bleeding, and I didn't know what was happening. She said, "Hush, you're a woman now." That's all she said, "You're a woman now. You have your period." I asked, what that meant, and no one really explained anything to me, except that somehow I can magically "make" babies. I'm now thinking, "Great. I just want to go back to my life playing, creating and having fun. My friends made it seem like it was all cool. It was all lies because, unfortunately for me, it was ugly, messy, dirty and I had to sit out during gym class, miss recess, and even miss school at times. If this was womanhood, I did not want it.

Looking back, I was a very sick child, and my mother was in and out of the hospital with me. I was born premature, there were complications, and I was in the Intensive Care Unit (ICU) in an incubator, where I was fed through a tube for about three months. My mother almost died during delivery. Her blood pressure was very low, and she had to remain in the hospital after giving birth to me. For the three months that I was in the hospital, she visited me every day. Being a premature baby, I developed other complications. I also had chronic anemia.

I was very tiny, very fragile and I was skinny as a child. Even though I ate a lot of different kinds of foods, I would never gain weight. At one point, I started to have common seizures, and I was diagnosed with childhood epilepsy. The seizures would come and go, and then they stopped. I had my last seizure at 10 years old, and I was hospitalized because I almost died.

Since I was a child, I've felt that God had His plan for my life, and a protective covering over me. The doctors knew that something wasn't right about my health. They couldn't come to a final diagnosis, but my mother was told that I would be taking medication for the rest of my life. My mother being the West Indian woman she is, believed that there had to be a holistic approach to my healing and me getting better, because my health was getting worse. Somehow, she was able to ween me off the medications the doctors had prescribed, by giving me different types of food and herbal remedies from the Caribbean. Some of the remedies she gave me included Cod Liver Oil pills, Liquid Iron and other supplements which I had to take on a daily basis. As a teenager, even though I had health challenges, it never affected my academic achievements. I was an all-around student, and was deemed a gifted child and one of the smartest students in the class - and in the entire school. I was put into a class for gifted children, and had a special curriculum.

Even though I was in and out of the hospital because I was sick, I did very well in Elementary School. After graduating Elementary School, I went on to High School, where I continued to be and all-around student who was active on the Student Council, went to Leadership Camp, and the famous Camp Olympia.

However, when it came on to that time of the month when my period started, I would miss classes, assignments and projects. Sometimes I would be away for a couple of days and sometimes weeks.

The teachers and others were concerned about missing classes, but they were impressed that even though I missed the classes, I was still able to keep my honour roll status right up to Grade 11. I was also involved in other activities like track and field and the drama committee, where I wrote and directed many stage plays. It was during this time I decided that I wanted to be a dancer, a Professional Artist. I had a dream! I started taking dance classes at school when I was 16, and started the Barbizon International Modelling School where there were competitions. This was all good, and I enjoyed it all. During this time, something happened.

As a teenager, who do we talk to about sex and other personal challenges. Most of the time, we go to our peers. Because I was always in pain, I shared this with my friends - and one particular friend recommended birth control. During my time in Grade 11 when I was 16 or 17, this friend and I decided to leave school in Etobicoke to go to a Sexual Health Clinic in downtown Toronto. We signed up to get free birth control which we received. With doing this, I felt like I was taking control of my own health. I started to take the birth control not because I was sexually active but to regulate my monthly cycle so that the pain would be minimized.

Unfortunately, shortly after this venture, this friend got into some trouble and had to take care of her personal matter. It's at that point, I realized that I too got into some "trouble." I was pregnant. I was given $200 and forced to have an abortion because I was in a relationship with an older man at that time. If it was known that I was with this man, it would have been statutory rape because I was under age, and at his age, he would have been charged so he made me have an abortion.

Fast forward to a couple of years later when I started a relationship and eventually got married. Unfortunately, I wasn't able to have children but didn't know why. At that time, my husband I and were living the good life. We were young Missionaries in church and worked on a part-time basis for a faith-based organization. We were living our lives!

I grew up attending a Catholic church. In my mind, I always tried to be the "good girl". I didn't want to be like my friends and other people around me. I wanted to wait until I was married to have children, and I didn't want to have multiple relationships. I really have to stress that the only reason I got pregnant is because I was taking birth control. I thought I was "safe" and didn't have to worry about getting pregnant. I was trying to finish high-school by graduating early and going to University. Unfortunately, that didn't happen. I got pregnant. That pregnancy led me to suffer with low self-esteem and guilt. My marks dropped drastically by about 3 or 4%. I was devastated. My family, especially my mother, was devastated. Because of this pregnancy, I left home when I was 18.

Chapter 2 - Clear Skies, Calm at Sea

I was assigned a Worker where I was living in a transitional home, a type of group home setting for young women who had run away from home. At that time, I decided that I wanted to be in law enforcement, but I knew that wasn't for me. I didn't want to be a Police Officer. However, I wanted to be a "Change Agent", so I became a Social Worker instead. I wanted to help young women like me. Through that program and living in that home, I was able to get a fully-funded college scholarship to go to school. I completed my diploma in Social Service at Centennial College Warden Woods Campus. Unfortunately, that Campus no longer exists. I had a great college experience.

Through my college experience, a friend of mine brought me to a Friday night meeting. He's like, "come let me take you to a meeting". I asked him why and he encouraged me to "just come". I went and it was "Tehillah Toronto", where young people gather and worship God. I've never been in that type of environment before. I told him how much I liked it and I continued to go each Friday night. I felt like God was tugging at my heart. I asked the question, "What can I do to get saved?" I grew up Catholic and was baptized as a baby, so I thought that I was "fine". However, I'm hanging around born-again Christians and they were telling me that I had to get baptized again as an adult. I spoke to a friend who was able to explain to me why it was important for me to get baptized again, as a born-again Christian. I committed my life to the Lord when I was 20, and I got baptized at 21. This began the journey. I got baptized in a local church closer to my home in Etobicoke. That's where I also met my husband. We were really good friends. He helped with my spiritual growth and development. I was fully into ministry and teaching children's church. I was a Youth Leader in the youth ministry, and I was taking kids to camp.

I was in Church almost seven days a week and that drew me closer to the man who helped bring me to the Lord.

We eventually got married. The one thing I can say is that looking back, I know at that time, I felt pressured and he probably felt the same way too. We were very young. Any advice I would give to anyone in their 20s is that you should "live your life, and focus on your goals and dreams." I had just finished college, and started working in a youth shelter. During this time, I lived in a transitional home. The shelter I worked at was Eva's Initiatives for Homeless Youth. These were young people who were at risk and ran away from home, just like me. The man who I was dating, at that time who later became my husband, was also a Child and Youth Worker. We were both Youth Workers and Counsellors. In ministry, we were Youth Leaders, who the church saw as "up and coming". We had good mentors and good people around us, who encouraged us to get married. Of course we felt pressured, but because a lot of young couples were getting married in the church, we decided to go ahead and get married.

I got engaged at 24 and got married at 25, but I definitely wasn't ready to get married. I was not ready to be a wife, nor was I ready to be a Pastor's wife. Hell no!!! I was never the "feminine" type. I was always into sports. I remember the first time I wore pants to church, as I never used to wear skirts. A lady came up to me and told me that I should be wearing skirt to church. I felt so embarrassed and told her that I didn't know that. She eventually helped to "mould" me into what was expected of ladies in the church. I also learned from the ladies in the choir and other ladies in the church, how to dress and conduct myself as a woman of God and a young lady in the church. I did accordingly.

I loved doing ministry but unfortunately, I wasn't ready to be a Pastor's wife. I accepted being able to preach, teach and travel. I still felt like an outsider being from another Island, attending a predominantly-Jamaican church. Even though I felt like an outcast as a Trinidadian, I still made friends and got involved in church. One day, I was asked by a young lady if I have ever danced professionally or if I have a "gift of dancing". They didn't know that I was a dancer. They just wanted me to join the worship dance ministry. I actually had never heard of worship dance. At 25, I started to do worship dance, and while they choreographed the dances, the Holy Spirit taught the full choreography and taught me how to use my body in worship, once I truly surrendered my life to God. I eventually branched out, because I wanted more. While visiting the Toronto Congress Center, I saw some ladies dancing and I decided that I wanted to dance on that stage. I later contacted Charmaine, the Director of Worship in Motion. I took some classes, got credited with dancing, started traveling with the group and became a member of the worship team. We got more opportunities to travel to Toronto, Ottawa, and to various churches.

It seemed that every time I'm on my period, and wearing that white dress, anxiety would set in and I would start to panic. I was worried that beautiful white garment I was given would get soiled. I remember being on 100

Huntley Street, in 2007. This was one of the biggest things that we had done across Canada. We had been on TBN networks across the US, but this was now National, as it was going across the country. That morning, my period came. If you look back at that video, I looked very sick because I was in so much pain. While I was in the dressing room, putting on my white garment, I was bleeding and praying, asking God to not let me embarrass myself. After getting dressed and having my make-up done, my fear was that this experience I waited my whole life for, would be ruined by that one thing - "the Red Lady", that "Lady in Red". Each month I felt like she was here to destroy me, and when I think that I am making progress, "The Lady in Red" comes to "wipe me out." Thank God we did a beautiful dance and got some great reviews. My life from the outside looked beautiful. My husband and I were recruited by Toronto Youth for Christ, where we were hired to be Youth Leaders. In Toronto, we were getting credentialed and licensed with Youth for Christ, where we could work with any Youth for Christ around the world. They sent us to a leadership program that was recruiting that year. Leaders from around the world would meet and get training in South Africa. We were able to raise funds and get sponsors, so that we could travel to South Africa. Of course my period came before we left. Let me say that it takes almost two days to get to South Africa. So, travelling on flights while on my period, wasn't something to look forward to. On the flight from Toronto to Paris, I was sitting in the middle seat beside a male passenger, and I had to go to the bathroom every 15-20 minutes. I just couldn't stay in my seat. It was the worst feeling, and I had to keep apologizing to the man. For our stopover in the Paris airport, I was able to get some tea, get all freshened and prepared for our trip from Paris to Senegal. I felt so sick during the flight, and this was the start of a 10-day journey in South Africa. I was so weak, and wasn't able to go the first session or orientation when we arrived in South Africa. All I could do is go to my accommodations and go to bed.

South Africa was great. It was one of the most spiritually-enlightening and special experiences of my life. I felt so close to God, that I tell everybody that God lives in Africa. I heard his voice clearly while working in Africa, and I knew it. I returned home with a higher purpose for my life; what I was going to do with my life, what I was going to do in the community, and what I was going to do with the youth ministry. However, there was one thing in my heart that I really wanted. The one area in my life that I wasn't "slaying" in, was me not getting pregnant. In the fall of 2008, I really wanted to get pregnant, but it wasn't happening. I was married for seven years, and was not getting pregnant. That devastated me.

I believe that one of the breakdowns in my marriage was because I couldn't get pregnant. I felt like most women would feel like "less than a woman", because they can't get pregnant for their partner. My husband already had a child so he was fine. He basically would have been happy with just having his son, but I wasn't because I wanted a little girl. I was going to the healing and deliverance ministries, seminars, and conferences every week, and I would be on my face crying out to God Asking where He was. I prayed for Him to open up my womb, to bless me with a child, because I wanted our family to be complete. I wanted a miracle baby, but it never happened.

Unfortunately, there were whispers among church members, church leaders, and even my own Pastor, who whispered into my husband's ear, telling him that it's because of my childhood and my sexual past, I was unable to get pregnant. One Pastor called and said that I have a "Jezebel Spirit" that I needed to be delivered from, and that I need to repent for my sexual past. I was very young and I didn't know what to do. I feel like I was coaxed into telling her my deepest, darkest secrets, and about being abused as a child. Her response was that all I shared with her were the reasons that I wasn't getting pregnant. During that time, all the thoughts went back to the last few years of my marriage.

My husband was so frustrated that when I had my appointment at the hospital, that he chose not to go inside with me. He dropped me off and never came into the waiting room with me. My appointment was for a blood test, which showed that I was anemic, and needed to get booster shots. Every three to six months, I had to go back to get an iron infusion. Sometimes my iron was so low, that I had to get blood transfusions. I felt really bad for my husband, because at that point, I don't think that he was fully cognizant of what was going on around him. I don't think he was competent as a man of God, and he was not ready for this type of battle. I'll tell you, he could pray, preach and could probably lay hands on other people and their lives change. For some reason, however, I don't know why he didn't believe in me, and it seemed extra hard for him to pray for me. Something was hindering him, and he basically gave up and probably saw me as "worthless" or a "wasted cause".

I honestly don't think that the problem was him, because I married my best friend, which means he knew everything about me. I honestly believe it's the people and the lies these people were telling. People would tell him these things in front of me, "She's psychosomatic". "She's bipolar." "Maybe she has mental health issues." "Something's wrong with that girl. Something's really wrong with her." And as you know, he believed. I needed him to stand strong as a Christian man. I needed him to fight. I understand from being outside of the situation, it was too much for him. I couldn't see clearly at that point. I couldn't imagine what he was going through from his point of view. The typical West Indian man would want his wife to cook, clean and take care of the kids. I was not that wife. He was the one that was cooking and cleaning, or getting help from his mother. I couldn't, I was just too exhausted. For a few years in my marriage, I would be bedridden at times and I couldn't do anything. I considered myself to be worthless, because I couldn't do anything. He would talk to other people and they would ask, "What kind of wife is that?" and tell him that he made the wrong decision. Even one pastor said to him, "Are you sure you made the right decision in marrying her? Maybe you should have married someone else or you should have waited." Somebody else told him that God would have had a bigger plan and purpose for his life, if he had just waited.

Friends who were close to me, told me that it was all in my head and that I was being "overly-dramatic.". This remark was one that I heard very often. It made me feel as though I wasn't ready to receive and that I had done something so wrong in my own life. Another woman told me that I was unable to conceive because I had sex before marriage. I believed them. As a young Christian, I did not know any better. In my early twenties, I didn't sleep around, yet I had felt completely worthless.

I could never compete. I could never be a perfect Christian, because the church had standards that I did not meet. Even though I was married, I wasn't producing a child - while all my other friends were getting married. By the time I left my ex-husband, some of my friends had two or even three children, and I didn't have one. I felt as though I didn't fit into the right category, or ideal mould of what a young Christian couple should be. We were supposed to be the next youth leaders - the next generation of pastors that they were teaching us to be.

People would often ask me, when was I planning to have a child. My mom would always say to me "You need to go get yourself checked out." It got to a point where I felt as though nobody had any faith in me – not even my own family. I had considered leaving the ministry, because my program, including the funding, was ending. Instead of continuing to ask for more funding, or a even a grant, I just quit the program entirely. I left the church and I left the ministry.

My life came to a halt. I felt a calling to go back into school and finish my degree. I was actually trying to dream again. What did I want to become? I wanted to become a teacher. Teaching didn't seem like it was going to be very stressful for me. I had decided to go to a Christian University College called Redeemer University, in Hamilton. I discretely applied to get an apartment, knowing that I was going to leave my husband. I just told him that I was going back to school. Eventually when I got clearance from the department, I moved, leaving my husband. I said to him, "I'm not leaving you. But I can't stay. If I stay here, then I'm going to die." So I left.

I even suggested that he could come up with me, but at that time he had gone to Tyndall University. We were both in the top two universities across Ontario. By that time, our goals and expectations had driven us apart. People had driven us apart. Church had driven us apart. Life had driven us apart. We were no longer intimate and we were sleeping on two separate beds. He knew at that point that there was no use in coming to rescue me.

I was just a lost cause. I also realized at that point, that I was actually married not to a narcissist, but to a person who is very controlling and manipulative. When I stopped doing what he wanted me to do in the relationship, I realized that's when it caused the most problems. I wouldn't call him a narcissist, but he has narcissistic tendencies in the way that he was very controlling and very demanding. I just stopped pretending to be that token, "trophy wife", as they call it. He just wanted to put me up on a pedestal. But he didn't want me to go anywhere. He didn't want me to wear any make-up. He didn't want me to wear nice dresses. He didn't want me to feel good. He would say to me, "You look like a whore. Go put on something more decent."

I left and then I applied for the separation .I was required to be legally-separated for one year. I was going to school at Redeemer, trying to complete two degrees. When I threw myself into school, I threw myself into activities to keep myself busy. I'm going to be a teacher, so I didn't have to think about anyone else. I left everybody. I left my family. I left my husband. I left my church. No one could get me to go into the chapel. One of the requirements for Redeemer University is every Wednesday you have to go to chapel.

I started to feel like there was something wrong. I never thought I could go back to my husband at that point. I could not go back to somebody who didn't believe in me, nor who never stood up for me or who never fought for me. When we took a vow, I believed him. I believed in the covenant and the sanctity of marriage. But I broke covenant and I suffered the consequences, but at the same time, I felt like he made me do that because he did not stand up for me. He did not cast away the lies and things that people were trying to say about me and he did not stand strong by my side. The very thought of me being in a relationship with a man that I mistrust, due to him not following through with his commitments and not being there for me in any way whatsoever, is very hard for me. I told myself that I would never get married.

I got no spousal support from my husband. He didn't try to support me or help me. I didn't receive OSAP funding that year, but he did. He finished university. I was not able to finish school. I couldn't pay for school and I had no way to go to school, so they took me out of classes. I was still living on campus, but only for the duration of my grace period.

So, I had dropped out of school. In 2013, they gave me a grace period to repay my loans. OSAP funding was supposed to come in September. I had already started my classes. In September and October, they sent me a letter, but I didn't receive it. I would not be able to continue; either they disenrolled you, or you dropped out. If I dropped out, I could always go back once I pay. But if they disenrolled me, then I would have to restart the process and apply for university all over again. I was allowed to temporarily stay on campus. I fell into a depression. I thought my ex-husband was stalking me; I wouldn't even feel comfortable enough to go outside. The only time I would go outside, was in the morning to go get my groceries.

I felt that he wanted to kill me, like he wanted to hurt me. I just wouldn't go outside. I would hide away and then I just couldn't take it anymore. I went into depression. Some friends tried to counsel me, but at that point in my life, I knew that I was going to take my life. I was going to commit suicide. I actually planned my suicide that Christmas, after I was planning to go home for the Holidays. Have Christmas dinner; go back after in the week of January. I was going to kill myself and let them find me in my apartment on campus. That was the plan. My nephew and his mother was away in Cuba. They left on December 22. My nephew said to his grandma, "I'm going to Ooba, I'm going to Ooba!" My mom said to him, "Have a good time in Ooba." They were only there for just over a day before my nephew was tragically struck and killed by a bus. He was only three years old.

My nephew died, so I couldn't kill myself now, because now we have to bury him. I didn't want to put my family through any more pain. I had planned it all; I was going to take painkillers and just slowly step into a pool. I tried to do that a couple of times in my life already. For some reason, I'm not sure if there's an angle or if somebody stood there at the wrong moment. I remember one time trying to do it, and it felt like somebody had stepped onto my chest. I wasn't able to move. I was paralyzed and I couldn't reach for the pill bottle.

Chapter 3 - Watch Out for Sharks

At this point, I have experienced many storms in life; Separation. Divorce. Betrayal. Trauma. Now, death. It was too much and I was drowning. I was drowning, and no one could save me. I thought no one or nothing could, but God. During that time, my nephew wasn't able to come back to Canada right away; it took him a couple of months first to get the body back to Canada and we were to have a proper funeral service.

Seeing that little child in the casket, just a little three year old boy and we couldn't see his face. We chose not to have an open casket, but I felt his hand, and his small hand was so cold. I said to him, "I'm going to live for you. I'm going to live. You did so much in your little life. You brought so much joy to people; you brought so much joy to me and to Auntie." God knows my deepest desire was to have a child. I didn't have a child, so I doted on my nieces and nephews. I doted on this little boy.

I'm going to look out for him. After everything, unfortunately I had to pack my things and move. Again, my family didn't know anything; they thought I just had started a new semester. Actually, this beautiful Italian family had been generous enough to offer to take me in. I slept on a couch, in their basement.

Some days, I just worked jobs, jobs and more jobs. I did temp jobs, just try to make ends meet. I also had a lot of tension with different men coming at me. I basically got involved with the wrong crowd and the wrong types of people. I found myself in a situation with men that would use and abuse me. Sex for me was just a transaction. I would use it to get anything I want. I felt horrible, but at that time, I just was in survival mode. I did what I could to survive. I didn't go to church, but I happened to continue to go to women's Bible study. I went during the week and I was faithful to that. I met these beautiful, kind-spirited women; I met some really good Christian friends again and most importantly I started to trust.

The woman were from all across Canada and were not the typical Black people who would try to interfere in my business or try to bad-talk me. I was introduced to many North American Christians, from different faiths and different backgrounds. They were so kind and loving. They were non-judgmental. I would share how I was feeling and what I had lost. They let me cry during Bible studies. They held me, they prayed for me. They just continued to believe in God for me. They were not my friends, but total strangers; yet somehow, God had used them. One lady would literally come and pick me up and after Bible study, we would go shopping. She would take me home and assured me I was cared for. *Now That's* the Body of Christ and I needed it at that time.

Up until this point, I had not felt that I was even worthy enough to step foot into a church. I was taught by the doctrines of the churches that I attended, that divorcees were not welcomed. Therefore, after my divorce, I never imagined that I could again be in ministry. Despite the fact that I had brought many young people and families to Christ and was a part of the restoration of their lives in the community, I still felt that I was not worthy. I kept far away from the people who I had helped, ministered to or prayed for. The true "Body of Christ" people assured me that I wasn't a lost cause and that God can still use me. I am not perfect, but I am worthy. I thought that I would never get to do worship dance again.

I would never dance again and I would never wear that white garment. I was not pure, as the church would say. Though God tells me that He still has a plan and purpose for my life. He is still using me. One day, I will dance again. He instilled in me, my heart's desire. He blessed me with the gift of dance and one day, I would use that gift.

All that I have done up until this point, brought me back to that one place. I was able to find peace, solitude, protection and safety at my women's Bible study. I continued to attend, no matter where I was or whatever I was doing. – and I still listened to the Word of God.

Despite all the running, the self-harm, and destructive activities that I got myself into, the only place that I felt safe was at my weekly women's Bible study. I started to slowly go back to church. When I attended church, the people there were not aware that I was. I was in-between houses, and in-between couches. I didn't have storage and the only thing I had was my gym membership.

I would go to the gym. I would shower there and I would change before church. I would leave my belongings there for a week, sometimes two weeks. As long as you had a lock, no one would interfere. The front desk saw me on a regular basis, but nobody knew that I had my things in the locker.

One time, I reached out to the pastor to tell him what I had been going through. He asked me whether or not I looked into social services or other organizations. At the time, there wasn't much that they could do to help, because I had no fixed address.

During that time, I met with what seemed to be a nice man who told me that he is a former pimp. I stayed with him for about two weeks. That time, I was very sick and I ended up in the hospital. He dropped me off to the hospital and I was told that I would need surgery. My father couldn't be reached or anybody else close to me.

After I left the hospital, being alone and vulnerable, the man took advantage of me sexually. I couldn't fight him off because I was on medication. I regained my strength, after leaving the hospital and I recovered on his couch. After my recovery, I just picked up my belongings and I left. I broke free. That was the last straw for me. I told myself, "Never again would I put myself in or end up in this situation."

Chapter 4 - Drowning, Someone Rescue Me

During that time, I was in an out of the hospital. I literally had to fight for my life. It got to the point where out of desperation, I had to threaten the surgeon by saying, "If you don't operate on me, I'm going to die. Something is seriously wrong. I need the surgery now." After seven times of being in and out of the hospital, they finally agreed to perform the surgery. However, it was scheduled for the following year, in January 2018.

I pleaded with them and told them, "If I don't have the surgery, I'm going to bleed out and die. I'm not going to live. Please, can we do the surgery this year?" My new gynecologist was a new doctor and made arrangements with another surgeon from another hospital. Thank God that she did that!

In October 2017, I had the surgery. I had a major surgery. They were also able to extract 16 fibroids and two large cysts. Unfortunately, there was a cyst that was still sitting on my Fallopian tube that they couldn't touch. But for the most part, they were able to get the scar tissue to test and see if their predictions were correct before they stitched me back up. I am blessed to have been born in Canada, where I can get the proper health care I need. Even though I had to fight for it. .

I only paid for the hospital fees, my room and my TV. The hospital staff told me that it would take four to six weeks for me to fully recover. Unfortunately, it wouldn't happen as smoothly. After my fourth week, when I met my gynecologist, she confirmed the results from the biopsy. I had stage four endometriosis and there was nothing they could do. She told me that I had two options, to be on medication for the rest of my life or to have a hysterectomy. She also told me that it would be extremely difficult for me to have children. My deepest fear was that I was infertile. The one thing I always wanted God to give me, was to have a baby.

My gynecologist said that if I were to have a baby, I would probably have to do it with IVF. I broke down and cried to my mother. My sister was with me at that time and I said to my sister, "You see? I was right! I knew something was wrong with me. I'm not crazy… All these years – I've always had this." I just cried. It was such a relief, like a weight that just came off of me.

Never mind that I had a six-inch scar going down from my navel, that I now had to live with. Never mind that I had to learn to walk again. Never mind that I couldn't bend and do certain things. But at least I could say, "Oh, I have a diagnosis. Now I know what I can do." They told me that there are holistic treatments that I can do to alleviate pain, but this pain would be with me forever.

Recovery was the hardest thing for me. Just imagine; after all of the pain and trauma that I caused my family, I now have to go back and live with the same people that I basically disrespected and disregarded. It's by my mother's grace she had to bathe me at 36 years old.

Somehow, God used that situation to restore our relationship and draw us closer together. The same child, the same baby who was fighting for that life in the incubator; my mother had to stand by my bedside, more than 30 years later to help my fight for my life again.

My mother is my strength. Every day she would come home from work and while she was making a meal, she would help me clean up. She just encouraged me and told me that I'm going to get better. She's the typical West Indian woman, you know. She's like, "You can watch me cook, but you know you can do something too."

My house was clean for her and my family when they got home. It gave me something to do and let me feel productive. When I got better, I was able to hustle, volunteer and do a little bit of work with an advocacy organization called Women's Health and Women's Hands.

Through that, I was also able to get my strength back and get my mobility back, though I was walking bent over. I had to fix myself, basically as well. I prayed and asked God "How do I do this?" The Holy Spirit told me that I need a plan and that I need a team of people. So in my mind, I said, "Okay, I need a team. Does that mean more help from the people that God has brought into my life, to help me recover and heal from the past traumas of my life?" Yes. Not only do they need to help me heal physically, but mentally, emotionally and spiritually. These are the type of people you need in your life; the type of people that the Holy Spirit was referring to.

So, I reached out to a friend and he connected me to a personal trainer named Gavin Skerritt Adams. I was able to start training with him at Phases Executive Studios, a private gym in Toronto. I did personal training and rehabilitation for about six months.

I used the feeling, the drive and the passion that I learned from working out. I used the motivation of going to the gym, to get up and get going. Even with that scar on my body. I took the bus and I walked very slowly to get there, but Gavin was always patient with me. He never pushed me beyond my limit, but he pushed me mentally. Eventually I was able to walk, run, be well and live normally again. If there's one thing that I could always say, it is that God does bring people in your life for a reason; I believe that he was one of them.

That thirst for fitness and working out are now rules in my life. I would love to train to do fitness modelling and do a competition one day. My trainer laughed, but he said "Whenever you are ready, call me."

Even though I was looking great and feeling better, I didn't really understand what endometriosis was. I went to the library, looked up information on Google and read books on it. I thought, "You know what; everything is great. I could just go back to my normal life, you know? I'm starting to date again and meet people again."

One thing that was very hard for me was sex for some reason. Intimacy was very, very painful. It's something that I continue to shy away from. As long as I could go without, I wouldn't do it; because who's going to want to do anything with me with the six-inch scar on my belly? I thought it was the ugliest thing. I was thinking that they'd have to be very soft with me – but I just shy away from that and any sexual intimacy. I just didn't want to have intimacy with anybody.

I said to myself, "No, I'm just done for now." Again, no one told me the things that I would go through. No one told me what I would have to do. However, I do believe in what the Holy Spirit told me, which was that I needed a plan and a team. I also started looking to other things to keep me busy and gradually starting to meet people. I couldn't even physically go in to resume full-time work at that time.

I assisted and volunteered at certain events in Toronto. Whenever a CEO or entrepreneur would ask me to work at their event, I would show up as a hostess or even as a greeter. I showed up in my best dress, best shoes, best nails and hair done. I showed up as if I was hired to work. I honestly thought that I wouldn't be able to work full-time again, but this was my side-hustle.

It looks like very unlikely. With the symptoms and the condition that I had, I developed even another chronic condition, with chronic anemia alongside with that. So basically every time I felt like a car running on empty fuel. There would be days where I get up early in the morning and feel so passionate and motivated; but by around noon, I was down and went back to bed.

Most of my days I actually spent in bed sleeping, napping and in-pain with my hot water bag and on medication. Unfortunately, during that time the medication that they gave me was weakening my liver and my bladder. I had contracted a very bad urinary tract infection.

I ended up back in the hospital. After being there for one week, my mother and I were advised by the doctor that I should stop taking a specific type of prescription drug, because it was damaging my liver and may lead to me being on dialysis. What neither of them knew, is that I probably being addicted to the medication. I continued to take the pills three to five times a day to numb the pain, numb myself and make me sleep. In a sense, I felt caught.

At that point, I said to God, "Please forgive me. I shouldn't have been taking all that medication. With everything that I've gone through - not being able to work full time, not being able to get my life back, not being able to be in healthy relationships." I felt that I wanted to be alone all of the time. I just felt very depressed. Just like sex before, medication was my comfort. So you see that I got myself back into an addictive lifestyle.

I overcame my temptations and I recovered from my addiction. I no longer took the pills. I thought God was telling me to get rid of those pills completely, because it was going to become the downfall of my life. The Holy Spirit told me to stop, or I'm going to die that way. I believed in Him. When I left the hospital, I stopped the pills cold turkey. Unfortunately, this sent my body into a rage. Without the pills, I would have to use food and other things to help alleviate my pain. I even looked into CBD oil and different rubs. While on this journey, I realized that one thing was clear. Through the stormy waters in my life, God was always throwing out an anchor. He was always throwing out that lifeboat for me to be safe and for me to call out for help because I was drowning.

Every single time I clutched onto that anchor to come back in, yet, somehow I ended up back in the water. After that, I continued to signal. I really needed to take control of my health and to control my life. I focused on doing the right thing and that started with me changing my diet.

I started to get rid of toxic people and situations by trying to live a healthy lifestyle. I believe in being situated in one church and staying devoted. I was putting my life back to God. As soon as I started to do that again, I saw a change in my levels of pain. I saw a change in my life, and I could do things.

I would 2019 was one of the best years of my life. I felt like I was living on a high and I was slaying in all areas of my life. I was able to work again, able to move and live to my fullest. I was in a new relationship and took up studying. I was good.

Chapter 5 - Clinging to the Rock

I found out Endometriosis is actually a genetic condition. In my family, supposedly my great aunt experienced symptoms, with very heavy periods. She unfortunately died and they had found a large cyst inside of her. My grandmother also had a heavy period. So did I, so it looks like it skipped a generation.

If had that knowledge as a young woman, I would have made smarter choices. My family and I would have sat down and discussed the best course of action to treat endometriosis at that time - more than twenty years ago. Birth control was the only the only thing that helped me to managed those types of symptoms..

I had basically found out about Endometriosis at thirty-six, and was already past my childbearing age. They told me that having a child right would be extremely difficult. I may take a couple of years and I would have to do IVF. I may have had multiple miscarriages before I have children. Now, at 39, I have to make a decision and ask myself whether or not I want to proceed to try to have a child. I read a stat that I may only have a 5 % chance of conceiving.

Even if I conceive at 40, it is possible for the child to be born with some sort of condition or deficiency. I do not want that to be the reality.

I know that God works miracles and I still believe in my miracle baby. I remember that God told me one year that by having a child I would birthing a promise. I know that one day, I will birth that promise. God even gave me a name for my daughter.

I'm standing firm on that. There are days where I wonder if it will happen. Days where it's hard for me to believe, but it has been twenty years since I've been able to conceive. There are times when the wise have given up hope. I said to myself, "Lord, am I like the woman in the Bible, Hannah."

How long would I have to wait for that child? How many tears do I have to cry, before I got that child? What would I have to do? Lord, I did ministry. Lord, I did everything that you told me to do. But yet, You still have not Blessed me with a child. For the benefit of my life, I still need to be healthier in order to actually carry a child full-term. I may not be physically, emotionally and even spiritually ready to be a mother. But in my heart, I'm already a mother. I know I'm going to be.

If I could go back and say to that 16-year-old or 17-year-old Stacy, to that young woman getting that birth control, I would have told myself to just wait. Get a second opinion. Talk to your parents, as hard as it is, about sex or what you're going through with your symptoms. Talk to your parents about going to the doctor. Try to stand up for yourself and be an advocate for yourself. It took me more than twenty years to advocate for myself. It took me having to go through a health journey and a near-death experience in terms of having to fight the medical system to give me a surgery, to advocate for myself.

Every woman should be taught at a young age to advocate for themselves, within the medical system. If they don't feel comfortable going to the doctors by themselves, then go with somebody that you can trust. Go with your family or go with a friend. In my case, many women are given limited options for treatment. If you are diagnosed with endometriosis, you either have to take this pill or you have to have a hysterectomy. No one should be forced to take either one of those options, unless they're totally comfortable and they know all the facts.

I didn't even know that I had that condition. So how could I find out the facts? Now that I know all of the facts, I'm telling you today, please speak to someone you trust. Speak to your doctors. Speak to a gynecologist. If they do not believe you, then get another gynecologist. If the doctor doesn't believe you, then get another doctor. But don't give up hope.

If you feel something in your gut that something is wrong with you, please seek the right help. If you continue to fight for yourself and advocate for yourself, you will see your way through any challenges. I want to tell those women today not to give up hope. It took seven to ten years for me to get diagnosed. At least I can say what's right for myself. Unfortunately, I had to lose my family. I had to lose my husband. I had to lose everything that I knew and leave my ministry behind. I'm still in pain every day, but if what it all lead to today, is that I am alive to tell you this story, then it was worth it.

In 2020, so many things have happened. COVID-19 has brought with it a global pandemic, with many experiencing the loss of their jobs, deaths worldwide, pain, trauma, storms and hurricanes. You could say the entire world is in chaos, but still standing somehow. During the pandemic, I never once ended up in the hospital. I remember bleeding for 15 days; I remember trying to get ahold of my doctor and couldn't access them online. I remember being on the same medication, for months after going into lockdown. I remember going to the grocery and not even seeing the right type of maxi pads or sanitary quantity that I needed to supply myself with during the pandemic.

Imagine being in Canada and not having that accessible. What about other young women around the world? What about young women living in Africa or in third-world countries? What about the young women in the Caribbean? What about the young women, who visit a doctor for a diagnosis or to undergo surgery and the doctor does not believe them? What about the young women who don't find out about their condition in time? They should not have to suffer when people choose not to believe their story.

Chapter 6 - The Perfect Storm to Take Me Out

Before the COVID-19 pandemic, I was supposed to start investigating in-vitro fertilization. I felt pressure from doctors, and everybody around me as I had endometriosis. The only way to basically subdue the symptoms and for you to feel better is "A", you have a hysterectomy, or "B", you get pregnant. I had a doctor that fully believed that if I got pregnant, that my endometriosis would go away and I would be fine.

After my first shot, I would be expecting, but that was not always the case. During that time, I was in deep prayer and fasting with my partner at that time. We had decided, to see what my options would be. Why this is so important to me, is that in my previous marriage, I was not able to conceive. At the time, I didn't even know that I was sick. I did not even know that I had a chronic illness and I didn't know that I would be suffering with fertility issues. Therefore, I didn't want to put another partner in that same situation; I didn't want someone to marry me not knowing if I would ever be able to conceive. So I just left all of my cards on the table. We had been in a relationship for two years at this point. I thought that if we were going to go forth, then we should at least know what our options are. He was supportive at the time, but he didn't want to go to the fertility clinic because he had apprehensions about the whole procedure.

I did not want to put pressure on him. But at the same time, I didn't want to deal with the reality of someone not knowing whether or cannot I can conceive. I said to myself, "Lord, this time I would be okay with knowing that I can't have a child of my own. Just please tell me." I would look into other options, other than freezing my egg.

Perhaps to adopt a child. My partner and I talked about that. We talked a lot about adoption. All of these paths require time and patience. As you can see, I am now in my late 30s and my clock is ticking.

He told me to just trust myself to follow through and take the fertility test. He said that it was my decision and asked me if the tests come back that I am unable to have children, if I would say that we can no longer be together. I said to him, "Yes." I thought at this point in my life, I had to make a decision. I had to make a choice and decide what I was going to do with my life.

I felt the Lord moving. When we were supposed to go in for the test, I felt the Holy Spirit say to me, "Wait, don't do it. Don't go." I came back to him and I said, "You know what? I think it's just better if we don't do it." At that time, I was going through a lot and I told him that there was no point of us being together. I got scared. I was disappointed that he didn't want to go to do the test with me, at first and I felt as though we had different expectations. I wanted to find a solution and I felt like he didn't want to find one with me. So, I said it was best for us to go our separate ways. I perceived that the relationship was done at that point.

In February and March, I would have been independent in doing those types of procedures. What would have happened, is that I would have lost thousands of dollars. I know and I hear stories of women who started in the clinic and were unable to finish. I can't imagine going through that type of stress. I thought of the type of feelings that those women would go through with their partners or husbands, at that time. I felt that God saved me and my partner from that. I can't even imagine that reality, but I know one thing is true; it would have definitely damaged my body and affected me not only financially, but physically, emotionally and spiritually.

It is my belief that you have to be very mentally-sound and in good health and spirit to go through something like IVF. Not everybody could do that. People stop or go through many cycles - and still no child. They spend $30,000 and still nothing. I can't image being on that end.

The side effects from taking those drugs leave your body in pain. Even though I prayed to my God that day, I had to lay down that plan. I had to put it down and stop thinking. I told my family that I wanted to have a hysterectomy. There are people around me who advised me to go and live my life.

Every person is different. I cannot say that a hysterectomy will work for everyone. I'm still looking for research in the health care of black women. But right now, there isn't a lot of information that I've found so far. All we knew is that black women tend to have more fibroids than Caucasian women and it can be passed down. It can skip a generation. My mother, aunt or cousin didn't get it, but I unfortunately did.

Chapter 7 - The Eye of the Storm

If it was not for my faith, I do not know where I would be today. Yes, I believe that God can heal, yet I also believe that we must each do our part. One thing that we do very well as Believers or people of faith, is that we mask our feelings well. We hide. We put on that face -the make-up, the hair, the nice outfit and heels and we put on a show Sunday morning. I should have won an Emmy for masking pain. I did it for many years - and this I believe how that darkness in my life slowly took me over. That darkness or eternal sadness was anxiety and depression. I was someone who was highly-functioning, but extremely sad and depressed.

The more I played dress up and ministered through dance, the more I felt like I the person I am was slowly deteriorating. Why couldn't I just be happy and have those feelings of joyfulness and glory that everyone was talking about. At one point, I had everything that I wanted; a loving husband, a thriving ministry and most importantly, a family. When I no longer had those things, I knew what I had been missing all along. I was looking for a sense of belonging, for acceptance and a place to finally call my home.

After all these years of running, I finally found my home – it is within myself. Right now, I am home and inside of me, I am more than enough. I don't have to pretend anymore and the mask has been ripped off. No one can make me happy - only me. Some women may come to this realization somewhere in their 30s. This *aha* moment can lead to some sort of mid-life crisis and may lead to a fight or flight response.

For those who are locked into their families, children, mortgages or investments, it's a little bit hard to flee. They may stay at the gym a little bit longer, in church a little bit longer or at the office a little bit longer. It's very easy to tell when a woman is not satisfied at home and when she is feeling stuck or fed up. For me, this happened at my Women's Bible Study. I was in a marriage and I felt stuck. I knew that I had to leave. I could not stay in a relationship that was stagnant and not growing or thriving and was basically dying after five years. I played the "good wife" role for as long as I could. I fulfilled my wifely duties and threw myself into my church ministry and dance activities. This kept me distracted. I thought that maybe things would get better, but it did not and my mental and physical health started to deteriorate. I burned out after five years of ministry, with nothing left to give. How can one serve from an empty vessel?

I tried to reach out to trusted individuals, I even went to couples marriage counselling by myself, because my husband at the time refused to go with me. He had his own demons that he was secretly batting with, that he never shared. Eventually, I found out after I had left him - but I felt in my mind, that I somehow did the right thing.

Up to this point, I've done individual counselling, some divorce counselling and cognitive behavioural therapy.

I've always tried to maintain routine sessions with a private Christian counsellor. Asking for help was the hardest thing for me, because that was my profession. It is what I went to school for; social work and counselling, especially crisis counselling. People like me are dangerous people to have on your chair or in your office. We know what to say and not to say, to make one believe that we are getting better when we are not. It isn't until we can acknowledge that we do not know it all and don't have all the answers - and only when we are ready to take responsibility for our own mess – we can see a change of heart or lasting transformation.

Forgiveness has been a key lesson for me. For years after my divorce, I was bitter. Sometimes, my skin crawls even at the mention of my ex-husband's name; but God has done great work to mend this broken heart. You see, my heart was already broken before I met my ex-husband. It was broken when my father and mother separated and divorced; it was broken when I was sexually-abused by a relative without any follow-up, therapy or acknowledgment. I was broken when I was seduced, raped and impregnated - then made to have an abortion to cover it up. Talk about skeletons in my closet.

The problem was that I never fully trusted men, because they always hurt or took something from me; so in turn, I would hurt them back. When there is no trust, there is no respect. I was abused, not just physically but in other ways - mentally, spiritually, and financially. It was easy for me to be verbally-abusive to other men, who could never meet my high expectations. My ex-husband said that it was very hard to love me. Hurting people, hurt people.

The best advice that I can tell someone, is to wait a bit until you have healed, before you go into a new relationship – especially after a separation or divorce. Trust me, the temptation is there, but the better you can heal, the more you set yourself up to be in a healthier relationship. You need a healthier you. I love you, sis! Take care of yourself. Self-care and self-love. Affirm yourself. Meditate, pray, exercise and change your diet.

Change your surroundings. Get rid of toxic people. Ask God for discernment to keep you away from predators, like narcissists while you are vulnerable. Don't be a victim and trust the process. Not everyone's story is going to be like the character from *Eat Pray Love*. The eye of the storm, they say is the safest place to be. Stay in God's will; and even if you get caught up, you will surely make it to the other side.

References

https://thehappypelvis.ca/racism-and-endometriosis/

https://endometriosisnetwork.com/blog/endometriosis-racism-how-the-strong-black-woman-stereotype-hurts-endo-patients